W9-DFV-087

DISGRACED!

The Dirty History of Performance-Enhancing Drugs in Sports™

COLLEGE ATHLETICS
Steroids and Supplement Abuse

ANNIE LEAH SOMMERS

rosen publishing's
rosen central®

New York

Published in 2010 by The Rosen Publishing Group, Inc.
29 East 21st Street, New York, NY 10010

Library of Congress Cataloging-in-Publication Data

Sommers, Annie Leah, 1968–
College athletics: steroids and supplement abuse / Annie Leah Sommers.—1st ed.
   p. cm.—(Disgraced! the dirty history of performance-enhancing drugs in sports)
Includes bibliographical references and index.
ISBN-13: 978-1-4358-5303-4 (library binding)
1. College sports—Corrupt practices—United States—Juvenile literature.
2. Athletes—Corrupt practices—United States—Juvenile literature. 3. Doping in sports—United States—Juvenile literature. I. Title.
GV351.S625 2010
362.29—dc22

                                                          2008055408

Manufactured in the United States of America

CONTENTS

Introduction

"**S**candal." The word itself sounds interesting. As much as people like to watch college sports, they like to read about the behind-the-scenes stories of athletes. It's even better when the word "scandal" shows up. People like to know that a star—be it a famous actor, a great musician, or an amazing quarterback—is human, too. Like everyone else, stars make mistakes.

In the United States, college sports are immensely popular. It's exciting to watch young athletes suddenly become heroes due to their talent, skill, and performance. We celebrate the idea of playing as hard and as fast as you can to be the best that you can be.

Unfortunately, winning at all costs has become the main goal in most sports. In order to win, many athletes are under increasing pressure to be stronger, faster, and just plain better. All too often, they turn to artificial means to improve their performance: steroids.

All steroids and many other performance-enhancing drugs (PEDs) are illegal to use without a prescription and/or banned by the National Collegiate Athletic Association (NCAA), the organization that governs college sports and makes up all the rules involving fair play. However, the desire to win is often so strong

The Florida Gators happily celebrate winning the FedEx BCS National Championship game. Winning without steroids and other performance-enhancing drugs is definitely the way to go.

that athletes, coaches, trainers, athletic directors, and even parents are often prepared to ignore the rules. This book is about those individuals.

When the truth of substance abuse comes out, reputations are damaged, as are students' futures, professionals' careers, and sports fans' faith in fair competition. As the NCAA continually strives to better educate athletes and others about the damage that performance-enhancing drugs can do, it's hoped that steroid scandals will eventually disappear from college athletics. In the end, winning naturally is the only way to go.

Chapter 1

School for Scandal

In the late 1980s, North America's leading sports news magazine, *Sports Illustrated*, published some shocking stories of steroid use that would forever change how the public viewed college sports. It certainly tarnished the image that many people had of young athletes trying their best. It also surprised many people who saw college coaches as role models dedicated to teaching such values as hard work, dedication, and team spirit. At the time, many sports fans were already aware of illegal substance abuse in professional sports leagues and the Olympic Games, but this was different. It was the start of a new era in college sports.

Getting Stronger: A Short History

The practice of relying on substances to increase strength, endurance, and performance goes back very far in history. Wrestlers in ancient Greece were known to eat huge amounts of meat to help them build muscles. Norse warriors ate hallucinogenic mushrooms before battle, believing this would make them better fighters. In 1889, seventy-two-year-old French doctor Charles-Edouard Brown-Sequard injected himself with fluid taken from the testes of guinea pigs. At a scientific meeting in Paris, France, he announced that the experiment had made him feel much younger and filled him with energy.

In 1935, nearly fifty years after Brown-Sequard's experiments, a German scientist named Adolf Butenandt developed anabolic steroids for medical

Long before their love of sports led to the creation of the Olympics, the ancient Greeks enjoyed boxing and wrestling. The creator of this piece of ancient Greek pottery from 530 BCE used images of these sports for decoration.

purposes. He even won a Nobel Prize for his groundbreaking work. Anabolic steroids build strength by increasing the body's level of the natural male hormone testosterone. This hormone is responsible for the development of typical male physical characteristics like large muscles, a deep voice, body hair, and testicles.

In 1954, a secret muscle-building recipe was passed on to John Ziegler, a team doctor for the U.S. national weight lifting team. A power lifting coach from the former Soviet Union told Ziegler that the Soviet team's winning streak was due to injections of extra doses of testosterone. Ziegler went to work creating

Before acting in big Hollywood action movies like *The Terminator* and becoming the governor of California, Arnold Schwarzenegger was known as a famous bodybuilder.

something similar. By 1958, he had succeeded. His anabolic steroid was called methandrostenolone. Ciba Pharmaceuticals manufactured it under the name Dianabol.

News of steroids' seemingly magical properties spread quietly but quickly, especially throughout the athletic community. By the early 1960s, team doctors and coaches had begun giving the new wonder drug to athletes. Most athletes had no idea that they were taking steroids—or even knew what steroids were. Some doctors and coaches treated the drugs as nutritional supplements or protein pills. Nonetheless, as steroid use increased throughout the 1960s, dangerous secondary effects began coming to light. Some of these side effects are psychological (in the mind), while others are physical.

In the 1988 Olympics in Seoul, Korea, sports fans were thrilled that sprinter Ben Johnson set a world record for his amazing performance in the 100-meter sprint. Sports fans everywhere were shocked when he was later accused of taking steroids.

By 1975, steroid use had become such a problem that the International Olympic Committee (IOC) added anabolic steroids to its list of banned substances. At the time, East German and Soviet athletes, in particular, were using steroids on a massive scale in order to become international champions. Just by looking at the athletes' monstrously bulked-up bodies and inflated muscles, it was obvious that something was going on. Despite the ban, steroids didn't disappear. This became apparent during the 1988 Olympics in Seoul, South Korea. The world watched in shock as Canadian sprinter Ben Johnson had his gold medal stripped after the anabolic steroid Stanozolol was detected in his urine sample after winning the 100-meter dash.

Steroid Side Effects

- Abuse of PEDs can stunt bone growth in adolescents
- Individuals who inject anabolic steroids with dirty needles are at risk of infection, including infection with HIV, the virus that causes AIDS.
- Men who use steroids often complain of "becoming more female," a result of some testosterone being converted into the female sex hormone estradiol. In some cases, male athletes need to have breast reduction surgeries.
- Steroids increase muscle mass. Carrying around too much weight can lead to ligament and joint damage.
- Users can exhibit strange, aggressive, and even violent behavior known as 'roid rage.
- In terms of appearance, users can appear bloated. Sometimes, they develop extra body hair. Other times, balding occurs. Severe acne is common.
- Long-term steroid use has been linked to liver damage, heart disease, and even heart failure.

Even though Johnson had been busted, his win was seen by many as an inspiration to follow his lead. On the Web site Steroidabuse.com, a former steroid user explained:

> For me, taking steroids was a natural move. I was an athlete in high school and got a college scholarship to play football at a major university. Between my senior year of high school and my freshman year of college, I started my first [steroid] cycle because I thought I needed to be faster. I took injectable testosterone and Winstrol [an anabolic steroid containing Stanozolol]. I figured that Winstrol must be good because it's what Ben Johnson got busted using. I wanted to be fast like him. I was getting stronger at every workout and feeling great. I had heard that steroids can make your joints weaker, but I figured Ben Johnson didn't have that problem, so it was probably just a rumor.

This anonymous athlete's statement is probably disturbing to most. However, it expresses a very common sentiment among supercompetitive young athletes: Get faster, stronger, and better—no matter the cost.

Chapter 2

The Tommy Chaikin Story

In the fall of 1983, a talented nineteen-year-old from Bethesda, Maryland, joined the football team at the University of South Carolina. His name was Tommy Chaikin. During his last year in high school, Chaikin was one of the best on his team. He had been named all-area, all-county, and all-metro. His reward: a college scholarship and an invitation to play college ball. It seemed like Chaikin was on the brink of becoming a great football player.

Fast-forward to South Carolina. His new team—the Gamecocks—was big, strong, and fast. While Chaikin was known on the team for being an easy-going guy, the other players were mean and aggressive and were always getting into fights. According to a few players' reports, some of the coaches even encouraged fighting. They believed that getting players worked up and angry made them more motivated to compete against opponents. As hard as he tried and pushed and worked and sweated, Chaikin found that he couldn't keep up with everyone else. The pressure to be a tough guy and excel was getting to him.

When Chaikin started playing college ball, it was 1983. The NCAA had yet to start a program testing for steroids, which would happen in 1986. In the meantime, student athletes were taking steroids and getting away with it. It was no secret to those involved that quite a few of the Gamecocks were taking performance-enhancing drugs. However, taking steroids meant that no one was playing fair. Even more important, the health of many promising college athletes was being put at risk.

A doctor holds a dose of human growth hormone. Although naturally produced by the body, some athletes take synthetic HGH because they believe it will help them perform better. HGH used this way can have negative health effects.

The Cat Was Out of the Bag

Fast-forward again to autumn 1988. The October 23 issue of *Sports Illustrated* had just come out. In it was the article "The Nightmare of Steroids," by sports writer Rick Telander and Tommy Chaikin. In it, Chaikin confessed that he had used steroids as a Gamecock in the spring of his first year. He also spoke out about the scandalous truth surrounding his experience with steroids and college ball. It was a serious wake-up call to the NCAA and the North American sports community. There was a lot of steroid use going on, and it was doing a whole lot of damage.

Unfortunately, steroid and supplement abuse is all too common in competitive bodybuilding, where the goal is to become as big and strong as possible. Above, a bodybuilder shows off his gigantic muscles at a competition in Kiev, Ukraine.

Having blown the whistle on the NCAA's first major steroid scandal, where does Chaikin fit into the whole story? Is he a victim of the system? Or, is he as responsible as his coaches? After all, what motivated everyone involved was a desire to win at all costs. In the *Sports Illustrated* article, Chaikin took responsibility for his actions:

I'm headstrong, and I've got a temper. I can't blame others for my mistakes, certainly not for making me take dangerous drugs. But I still think of myself as someone who started out as just a normal guy, a hard worker, a studier, a kid who loved sports. And I feel part of the trouble

Bad Career Move

Nineteen-year-old Jared Foster, a former Mississippi high school football star, was arrested for trying to sell anabolic steroids to an undercover policeman in October 2007. The 6-foot-5-inch (195.5 centimeter), 215-pound (97.5 kilogram) quarterback was expected to excel at the college level. However, because of his arrest, Foster lost his scholarship to the University of Mississippi. He was given a five-year sentence and fined $5,000.

comes from things outside of me—the pressures of college football, the attitudes of . . . coaches and our just-take-a-pill-to-cure-anything society.

Should the coaches shoulder most of the blame for endangering the health of their players? They certainly didn't try to dissuade Chaikin from doing drugs. In fact, in the *Sports Illustrated* article, Chaikin recalled that before he had made the decision to start using steroids, one of his coaches encouraged him by saying, "Do what you have to do. Take what you have to take." As a result, Chaikin went from being an honest athlete ("I was going to build myself up naturally," he said) to a competitive player who allowed his pride to get the best of him.

The Results of 'Roids

At first, Chaikin was pleased with the results of the steroids. His muscles grew, he could lift a lot more in the weight room, and he had tons of energy. The coaches seemed to be pleased with him, too. They were no longer on his back about becoming a more aggressive player. However, Chaikin found himself dealing with a lot of negative side effects. Often, he was anxious to the point of being sick. Sometimes he was so aggressive that he'd scare himself. There were times when he would become so furious that he would start seeing red. Then he developed high blood pressure and a heart murmur. He couldn't sleep properly. Often, on the nights when he couldn't sleep, he'd drink quite heavily. He also had acne all over his back, and his hair was falling out.

But aside from these health problems and symptoms of 'roid rage, Chaikin felt as though no one could possibly beat him. He was strong and mean, and he was playing really well. He would play against guys who would huff and puff, and Chaikin wouldn't even feel winded. Then it seemed like things were getting out of hand. He was worried about some of his behavior. He got into fights at bars. He was becoming paranoid. Once, Chaikin was so aggressive, he got into an

Football is the most popular college sport in the United States. The University of Southern California football team, the Trojans, work on their skills at a spring practice game at the Los Angeles Memorial Coliseum.

argument with one of the team's trainers and put his hand through a metal locker, ripping the door from its hinges. His nerves were on edge like never before. Then things got even scarier. As Chaikin recalled in the *Sports Illustrated* article, "I was sitting in my room at the roost, the athletic dorm at the University of South Carolina, with the barrel of a loaded .357 Magnum [gun] pressed under my chin. My finger twitched on the trigger."

Chaikin had had enough. He called his family who, luckily, came to the rescue. The drugs he had taken had done too much harm. All of a sudden, winning wasn't worth it. Ultimately, Chaikin was hospitalized and was on the road to getting clean. A few months later, his story would be published. He hoped it would prevent other student athletes from having similar experiences.

The Details

Unfortunately, anabolic steroids were not the only questionable substances being used by college football players. Another performance-enhancing drug that had begun to gain popularity in the sports circuit was human growth hormone, known as HGH. Produced by the pituitary gland, HGH occurs naturally in human beings. It is responsible for increasing muscle mass and lowering body fat. However, in some cases, the body doesn't produce enough HGH on its own. This can be serious for growing children and elderly people. In such cases, doctors sometimes prescribe manufactured HGH to increase muscle strength. When its benefits were discovered, HGH became popular with athletes. A big advantage was that it wasn't considered to be a steroid, and it was not a banned substance. Like steroids, however, HGH can have dangerous secondary effects if used improperly.

In the *Sports Illustrated* article, Chaikin recalled his first experience with HGH:

[While] [s]ome bodybuilders take $10,000 worth of HGH per cycle [a bodybuilding term used to describe taking a series of drugs, over time, in varying doses] . . . I only got $800 worth, enough for 10 injections over eight weeks . . . My attitude was: Just give me what it takes to get big.

Of course, "what it takes" is never enough. Chaikin continued:

This competitor at the 2008 Berlin Bodybuilding and Fitness Championships flexes for the judges. Many people ignore the dangers of steroids in pursuit of a muscle-bound body.

My supplier told me that if I didn't get too crazy with this stuff, didn't abuse it, I'd be OK. Then, we went down into his basement at home, and he gave me my first injection, in the top of my butt. I went right to the weight room and had a great workout. I was pumped . . .

Chaikin's description of how the substance works is like Clark Kent suddenly turning into Superman or David Banner morphing into the Incredible Hulk. After shooting up, his muscles swelled. Chaikin found that he could work out much harder than usual because his muscles didn't get fatigued as quickly. This muscle growth enhanced some of the psychological effects of the drug, a major one being aggression.

Also in the article, Chaikin told of how he had gone home to visit his family during spring break. His mother took one look at him and said, "What have you done to yourself?" His father had tried to talk him into quitting and had involved their family doctor. Chaikin wasn't ready to quit. As his third varsity season progressed, he became quite sick. Still, he kept juicing up. In the summer of 1987, his anxiety attacks got worse. Soon he ended up with the gun in his hand.

Speaking out in *Sports Illustrated* had helped put a stop to what was going on at South Carolina. Ultimately, defensive coordinator Tom Gadd, defensive line coach James Washburn, tight end coach Tom Kurucz, and strength coach Keith Kephart were all charged in connection with distributing steroids to Chaikin and some of his teammates, from 1984 to 1987. U.S. Attorney Vinton D. Lide, who prosecuted the matter, did not charge the players with any crimes—he considered them to be victims.

Chapter 3

Winning Ugly

The NCAA started testing for performance-enhancing drugs and anabolic steroids in 1986. However, college athletes were not tested often. Originally, the NCAA tested only at championship games and meets and at football bowl games. It wasn't until 1990 that the NCAA expanded its program and began testing throughout the school year (from August to June). It would be another few years before testing during the summer would begin. Also in 1990, the U.S. Congress passed the Anabolic Steroid Control Act. Tommy Chaikin's story greatly influenced its passage. The Steroid Control Act classified steroids as addictive and dangerous substances. Without a doctor's prescription, selling or otherwise distributing them became an offense that could be punished with up to five years of prison time.

Lyle Alzado: "It Wasn't Worth It"

Like Chaikin, football star Lyle Alzado went public about his steroid use in an article in *Sports Illustrated*. Alzado's story was published in July 1991, shortly after he had been told that he had a rare kind of fatal brain cancer. Though he had once starred in the NFL, he was in terrible shape. Only forty-two, Alzado was balding and was barely able to walk. He had trouble remembering things, but he certainly couldn't forget the regrets that he had about taking steroids.

In his article, titled "I'm Sick and I'm Scared," Alzado shared a strong message about using steroids: "It wasn't worth it . . . If you're on steroids or

Lyle Alzado (*left*) of the Los Angeles Raiders attempts to tackle running back Sammy Winder of the Denver Broncos during a 1984 season game. Alzado was a steroid user during his time with the Raiders.

human growth hormone, stop. I should have." Unfortunately, it was too late for Alzado. Less than a year later, he was dead. As writer Mike Puma at ESPN.com wrote, "Although there is no medical link between steroids and brain lymphoma, Alzado was certain the drugs were responsible for his cancer. He became a symbol of the dangers of steroid abuse."

How did Alzado end up so ill? He admitted that he had started taking anabolic steroids while still in college, in 1969, well before they were banned. In an article about the NFL's strongest men, ESPN writer Shaun Assael described how Alzado was always "painfully insecure about his body since he was a 190-pound (86 kg) kid in Brooklyn. It's why he started popping Dianabol at Yankton College in

In the last painful months of his life, Lyle Alzado became a spokesperson for the grave dangers of steroid abuse. Alzado was one of the first major athletes who admitted to using steroids to boost his performance.

South Dakota while turning himself into a 300-pound (136 kg) QB killer who didn't just threaten the lives of opposing linemen, but those of their kids."

In "'Roid Rage," an article for ESPN.com, Mike Puma reported that Alzado said he spent four to six hours daily in the weight room at Yankton. He went from 195 pounds (88 kg) as a freshman, to 245 pounds (111 kg) as a sophomore, to 280 pounds (127 kg) as a junior, and ended up tipping the scales at 300 pounds (136 kg) as a senior. Alzado became the first player drafted from Yankton by an NFL team. In his article "Not the Size of the Dog in the Fight," ESPN's Puma stated plainly, "Lyle Alzado's ticket to the NFL was anabolic steroids."

The Ugly Truth: What the Specialists Have to Say

- In a *Deseret Morning News* article written by Dick Harmon, longtime University of Utah trainer Bill Bean recalled the results of a survey conducted by the U.S. Olympic Committee. The survey asked young people if they'd be willing to ingest a harmful drug if it meant that they'd have a greater chance at winning an Olympic medal. This hypothetical substance would be dangerous, perhaps even fatal, to the athlete who took it. Despite such grave risks, the majority of those surveyed were willing to try the drug.

- Dr. Gary Green, a specialist in sports medicine and chairman of the NCAA Drug Test Committee, summed up the lure of steroids when he noted on DrugStory.org, "The problem is steroids 'work.' You do get bigger. You can train harder."

With the help of steroids, Alzado moved on to the NFL, having been drafted by the Denver Broncos in 1971. "My first year with the Broncos, I was like a maniac," Alzado recalled on ESPN.com. "I outran, out-hit, out-anythinged everybody." It seemed like a promising beginning to a great professional football career. However, in reality, it was the beginning of two decades of cheating and lying. Eventually, steroids took a toll on his career and on his health.

Tons of fans watch the Michigan State Spartans—Tony Mandarich's former team—play a football game at home in East Lansing, Michigan.

The Numbers Game: Tony Mandarich

While the cost of PEDs is amazingly high, so is the cost of testing. The NCAA pays around $4 million a year for testing. However, despite the NCAA's best intentions, some coaches and athletes have become experts at beating the system. Even some of the most promising athletes have found themselves abusing steroids to keep up their winning ways.

Back in 1989, Tony Mandarich was a 6-foot-6-inch (198 cm), 315-pound (143 kg) football player at NCAA football powerhouse Michigan State University. Over his college career, Mandarich did his school proud, proving himself to be an exceptional athlete. Apart from playing in the 1988 Rose Bowl, Mandarich was named a first-team All-American and was a two-time Big Ten Lineman of the Year. In an interview with *Sports Illustrated* in April 1989, Michigan State head coach George Perles said: "He may be the best offensive tackle ever . . . He's faster than any offensive lineman in pro football. There's probably nobody faster in the world at his weight. This is a different player. We'll never have another."

Aside from lifting weights morning and night, Mandarich ate seven meals totaling 12,000 to 15,000 calories every day in order to stay at the top of his game. However, his game performance was so impressive that many people also wondered if he was using steroids. Those who knew him claimed that such accusations were ridiculous. After all, Mandarich had passed the three drug tests that he had been given: one before the 1988 Rose Bowl, one before the 1989 Gator Bowl, and one at an NFL-sponsored scouting event. Those in his inner circle—including his brother and parents—totally supported Mandarich's claims that he was "clean."

In October 2008, the truth finally came out. Mandarich appeared on Showtime's *Inside the NFL* program and admitted that he had taken steroids during his career. Soon after, he spoke to *Detroit Free Press* reporter Shannon Shelton. When asked if the Michigan State University Spartans had questioned his steroid use, Mandarich told Shelton that he just "denied it." Was this a tough thing to do? "It was easy," he said. "I cheated on one test, but in my five years at MSU, I was only tested five times. There was no test when we went to the Cherry Bowl. At the All-American Bowl, I got off the drugs and got clean before I went to Birmingham, Alabama, and had to take the test. We didn't go to a bowl in my junior year."

According to Mandarich, he was tested twice before the Rose Bowl in 1988. Again, he got off drugs and went clean and passed the first test. But then there was a surprise test, and he had to resort to cheating to pass the second test.

Testing Troubles

Tony Mandarich's story is proof that, despite good intentions and the large amounts of money spent, testing for steroids and other PEDs isn't always that effective. As Mandarich confessed in an interview with Rob Longley of the

A chemist is hard at work at UCLA's Olympic Analytical Laboratory. This is one of the laboratories that is used for NCAA drug testing.

Toronto Sun following his retirement, "I can't tell you how many drug tests I have taken in the NCAA, in Bowl games, and in the NFL, and I've never tested positive for anything."

So, how is it that the NCAA did such a poor job? NCAA schools are informed about testing up to forty-eight hours ahead of time. This advance warning allows cheaters plenty of time to devise ways to get around the test. For example, some athletes have submitted someone else's clean urine sample. They may keep the specimen in a container in their armpit, releasing it through rubber tubing that they run into their pants. If a sample collector does not follow procedures, this fake sample may work. Dishonest athletes from all sports try all the time to beat the tests. A December 2003 article in *Sports Illustrated* discussed an incident involving a bodybuilder who tried to fool a test collector by handing him a fake urine sample. The collector was worried about the health of the bodybuilder when he saw oil floating in the sample. As it turned out, the muscleman had emptied out an old suntan lotion bottle, filled it with water, and taped it between his legs.

Chapter 4

Some Kind of Role Models

Although some of them may seem larger than life, it's important to remember that the athletes who dazzle us with their performances in college sports are often still teenagers. Their age and lack of experience mean that they count on adults in authority positions for guidance and direction. After all, the things they have to deal with—both on and off the field—are enormous. Young players have to deal with the constant pressure of making tough decisions, performing well, earning (and not losing) scholarships, and impressing pro scouts. And let's not forget peer pressure. For these athletes, their entire future may be riding on how they perform in college.

Players spend hours each day in the company of their coaches and trainers. Many serve as role models, especially for athletes who, for the first time in their lives, find themselves far from home without any parental figures around. Coaches and trainers often become substitute parents, adults who can be trusted to help with problems and offer guidance and support. You would think that they would have the best interests of the younger generation in mind, and the majority of them do. Yet, coaches and trainers also have a lot of pressure on them. They have to worry about where their careers are going. And if they want their careers to move forward, they have to make sure that their teams are going to win. Unfortunately, just as for the players, sometimes these pressures are so great that some coaches and trainers get carried away and make bad decisions.

Older athletes who are drug-free are great role models for student athletes who have less experience and are easily influenced. A game not often associated with steroids is soccer. Here, the USA Men's National Team practices.

Adults Leading the Wrong Way

One of the first big steroid scandals in college sports started with a mysterious death. On October 19, 1985, twenty-three-year-old track and field star Augustinius Jaspers was found dead in his dorm room bed at Clemson University in South Carolina. Nobody could imagine what had caused the death of such a healthy young athlete. However, a subsequent autopsy found that Jaspers had a congenital heart disease, as well as small amounts of a performance-enhancing drug called phenylbutazone in his blood. Three capsules of the drug, used to help upper-body muscles grow quickly, were then found in Jasper's room. Though authorities could not be certain that the drug killed him, the incident was the start of a major investigation that would spread throughout the country. In the meantime, everyone was trying to figure out how the young athlete got the PED in the first place. Since Jaspers did not have a prescription for the drug, someone must have given it to him. But who?

In January 1985, *Sports Illustrated* ran an article, "A Pipeline Full of Drugs," that brought the story to the general public. In the article, author Bill Brubaker tells how the trail eventually led to Sam Colson and Stan Narewski. Colson was Clemson's strength coach and the women's track and field coach. The other suspect, Narewski, was the men's track coach. Then, there was E. J. (Doc) Kreis, the Vanderbilt University strength-and-conditioning coach.

A Web of Suspects

Other clues led to a man named M. Woody Wilson. Wilson was pharmacist, a medical professional who has the authority to make up prescriptions and sell them to people—but only under a doctor's orders. In Wilson's case, however, there weren't any doctor's orders. Ultimately, the authorities discovered he had been selling steroids and phenylbutazone without a prescription to athletes at Vanderbilt University for more than two years. He also sent the drugs to Kreis and Sam Colson. In an article published in the *New York Times* from January 20, 1985, Arzo Carson, the director of the Tennessee Bureau of Investigation, estimated that Wilson had sent close to five thousand doses to Colson. Colson admitted to investigators that he gave some of the drugs to Narewski, who then gave them to Jaspers.

The Candy Man

In 2003, the University of Washington began investigating a doctor known as the "Candy Man." William J. Scheyer was a team doctor for many of the University of Washington's sports teams, including football, track and field, softball, and men's basketball. Scheyer had been in practice in Washington since 1959. A sports medicine specialist and surgeon, he ran the Washington Sports Medicine

Institute in the town of Kirkland. What many people didn't know, however, was that over the years, Scheyer wrote hundreds of prescriptions and gave out thousands of doses of anabolic steroids, narcotics, sedatives, stimulants, and tranquilizers to student athletes. According to state health officials who investigated Scheyer, his method was to order the drugs from local pharmacies, remove them from their original pharmaceutical packages, and put them into small white envelopes with handwritten instructions on them. Scheyer distributed these drugs to athletes before, during, or after training sessions or at athletic events. He also gave a supply to team trainers to take on road trips to games and meets at other schools. Scheyer became known around campus as the "Candy Man" and "Dr. Feelgood."

Several coaches and university officials knew about Scheyer's schemes. According to an April 28, 2004, article

Barbara Hedges announced her retirement in the wake of the Scheyer steroid scandal.

in the *Seattle Post-Intelligencer,* some softball players said their coach, Teresa Wilson, told them to "go see Dr. Scheyer and get whatever they needed from him." (Washington has one of the premiere women's college softball programs in the country.) One player remembered being so high when on the medication that she was rolling on the dugout floor and laughing. Others resisted taking drugs but were afraid to talk about their concerns to their other coaches or those in charge of the athletic program.

Following the investigation in 2003, it was found that these drugs had been given to athletes with no regard for their safety. Wilson and the athletic director,

Texas A&M faces off against Arizona State in the NCAA Women's College World Series Finals in 2008. Female college athletes seem to have fewer problems with steroid and supplement abuse.

Barbara Hedges, were criticized in the panel's report for doing nothing about Scheyer's dangerous activities. Wilson denied any wrongdoing but was removed as coach. Hedges retired. Meanwhile, Scheyer agreed to surrender his medical license in 2004. According to UW president Lee Huntsman, worse than the disgrace the scandal brought upon the UW athletic program was the fact that students' health had been put at risk. Said Huntsman in a 2004 press conference, "We failed [to keep students safe], and this to me is deeply troubling and painful. We will try to do better."

Chapter 5

Trying to Make the Grade

n May 2008, ESPN.com gave out grades to the NCAA, the National Football League (NFL), the National Basketball Association (NBA), and Major League Baseball (MLB) as a way of rating how effective their drug-testing policies were. They were measured against the gold standard of testing—the Olympics. The NCAA received only a "C." What this means is that even when testing is in place, it's not always a foolproof way of monitoring steroid use.

What About the NCAA?

There are plenty of critics who think the NCAA could do a lot better. A major complaint is that the NCAA chooses to test schools instead of individual athletes. And it wasn't until June 2006 that student athletes were tested in the summer, which is when many athletes actually take lots of performance-enhancing drugs. Even so, testing done over the summer was random and involved only a select few athletes in each sport. Because the NCAA often informs each school about the testing up to forty-eight hours before the testing crew shows up, steroid-dependent athletes have plenty of time to cheat. If school officials suspect an individual athlete of using illegal substances, their only solution is to bring in private testing, which can be extremely expensive.

Testing aside, many athletes these days rely on so-called masking agents. These are supplements or medications—which are neither banned nor

Testing ABCs

At the beginning of the school year, NCAA student athletes have to sign a form agreeing to be tested for drugs. A list of banned substances is attached to the form so that they know what they are not allowed to take. If the form is not signed by the deadline, the athlete will not be allowed to practice or compete until the form is handed in. An athlete who signs the form at the beginning of the year but then fails to show up for an actual drug test is banned from competing for a year.

illegal—that live up to their name because they mask the steroids in your body. Sometimes, they do this by flushing the steroids out of your system. Afterward, there is such a small amount of steroids present in the urine that test results come out negative. Even without masking agents, many athletes bank on the odds that they will never be tested. The ESPN.com survey noted that at the top Division I schools with football programs, only eighteen players are tested each year. If a school doesn't have a football program, the number of students being tested is even smaller. In this case, only eight athletes are chosen and tested out of the entire population of athletes.

Fighting Back

In 2006, an NCAA research committee released a report on the past five years of steroid testing. The report showed that the number of college athletes who tested positive for steroids dropped 47 percent from 2000 to 2005. Jerry Koloskie, the committee chairman, said in an NCAA news release from

The only way to determine if an athlete has been taking performance-enhancing drugs is to test for them. These vials, seen at UCLA's Olympic Analytical Laboratory, contain specimens that have been tested for artificial compounds.

July 6, 2006, "These results are really encouraging and are the direct result of an on-going partnership between the NCAA and member institutions to continue to strengthen drug testing efforts by providing education and awareness programs." Koloskie was referring to programs that warn student athletes about the negative consequences of using steroids and other PEDs.

An NCAA research survey given to student athletes in 2005 also showed that there was a noted decrease in steroid use. This is a national study that has been conducted every four years since the initial test in 1985. Statistical trends since the 2001 survey included:

One of the most common ways of cheating on steroid testing is to falsify a urine sample.

- A decrease in the number of student athletes who used anabolic steroids to help treat an injury
- A decrease in the number of users who stated they had used steroids to improve their physical appearance
- An increase in the number of students who felt that the NCAA testing had helped keep athletes drug-free

Fighting steroid use in college sports is a tough battle, but it's important to keep trying. The results of the NCAA study are a great example of the good that comes from increasing knowledge of the dangers of steroids. It's not only

College athletes don't have to break the rules to make it to the top. Here, Xavier Omon leaps over defenders during a 2007 NCAA Division II championship football game. Omon went on to play for the Buffalo Bills.

up to the schools. Schools, parents, and student athletes can help a great deal by being aware of and talking about a lot of the issues that student athletes face. Most important of all is that young athletes should be aware of the dangers and harm that can come from using these substances.

GLOSSARY

anabolic steroids Testosterone-based drugs sometimes used by athletes to help increase weight and strength.

autopsy Examination of a dead body to discover the cause of death.

bloated Swollen.

circuit An association of people or groups.

endangering Creating a dangerous situation.

hallucinogenic Impacting the mind to the point of creating vivid visions.

human growth hormone (HGH) Hormone naturally produced by the pituitary gland that increases muscle mass and lowers body fat.

intention The desire to achieve something.

ligament Band of tissue that connects bones and holds organs (like the liver and kidneys) in place.

Nobel Prize Special award, named after Alfred B. Nobel, that is presented every year to people who make great achievements in such fields as physics, chemistry, medicine, literature, and peacekeeping.

prescription Written direction from a licensed physician to take a certain drug or medication.

specimen Sample (of blood or urine, for example).

supplements Vitamins, minerals, and other substances taken in addition to what the body normally requires.

tarnish To spoil or diminish.

FOR MORE INFORMATION

American Medical Association (AMA)
515 N. State Street
Chicago, IL 60610
(800) 621-8335
Web site: http://www.ama-assn.org
The American Medical Association helps doctors provide service to patients by
    bringing together physicians nationwide to work on important health issues.

Association Against Steroid Abuse
521 N. Sam Houston Parkway East, Suite 635
Houston, TX 77060
Web site: http://www.steroidabuse.com
This organization works to educate and protect against the abuse of anabolic
    steroids by providing information to athletes and young people, as well as
    parents, educators, and sports organizations.

Canadian Interuniversity Sport (CIS)
801 King Edward, Suite N205
Ottawa, ON K1N 6N5
Canada
(613) 562-5670
Web site: http://www.interuniversitysport.ca
The CIS is the equivalent of the NCAA in the United States, overseeing all aspects
    of Canadian university-level athletic competition, including doping control.

National Center for Drug Free Sport, Inc.
2537 Madison Avenue
Kansas City, MO 64108
(816) 474-8655

Web site: http://www.drugfreesport.com

Drug Free Sport provides alternatives to traditional drug-use prevention programs for athletic organizations.

National Collegiate Athletic Association (NCAA)

700 W. Washington Street
P.O. Box 6222
Indianapolis, IN 46206-6222
(317) 917-6222
Web site: http://www.ncaa.org

The NCAA is a voluntary organization through which the nation's colleges and universities govern their athletic programs.

National Institute on Drug Abuse (NIDA)

National Institutes of Health
6001 Executive Boulevard, Room 5213
Bethesda, MD 20892-9561
(301) 443-1124
Web site: http://www.nida.nih.gov

A branch of the National Institutes of Health, NIDA is the world's largest supporter of research on drug abuse and addiction.

National Institutes of Health (NIH)

6001 Executive Boulevard, Room 5213
Bethesda, MD 20892-9561
(301) 443-1124
Web site: http://www.nih.gov

The NIH is the federal agency dedicated to medical research. Its scientists study the causes, treatments, and cures for common and rare diseases.

World Anti-Doping Agency (WADA)
Stock Exchange Tower
800 Place Victoria (Suite 1700)
P.O. Box 120
Montreal, QC H4Z 1B7
Canada
(514) 904-9232
Web site: http://www.wada-ama.org/en
The WADA is involved in coordinating, monitoring, and working to prevent the
use of PEDs in all sports throughout the world.

Web Sites

Due to the changing nature of Internet links, Rosen Publishing has developed
an online list of Web sites related to the subject of this book. This site is
updated regularly. Please use this link to access the list:

http://www.rosenlinks.com/dis/coll

FOR FURTHER READING

Aretha, David. *Steroids and Other Performance-Enhancing Drugs*. Berkeley Heights, NJ: MyReportLinks.com Books, 2005.

Crist, James J. *What to Do When You're Scared and Worried: A Guide for Kids*. Minneapolis, MN: Free Spirit Publishing, 2004.

Crutcher, Chris. *Deadline*. New York, NY: HarperTeen, 2007.

Deuker, Carl. *Gym Candy*. Boston, MA: Graphia, 2008.

Lau, Doretta. *Incredibly Disgusting Drugs: Steroids*. New York, NY: Rosen Publishing Inc., 2008.

Mintzer, Richard. *Steroids = Busted!* Berkeley Heights, NJ: Enslow Publishers, 2006.

Monroe, Judy. *Steroids, Sports, and Body Image: The Risks of Performance-Enhancing Drugs*. Berkeley Heights, NJ: Enslow Publishers, 2005.

Murdock, Catherine. *The Off Season*. Boston, MA: Graphia, 2008.

Schaefer, Adam Richard. *Health at Risk: Steroids*. Ann Arbor, MI: Cherry Lake Publishing, 2008.

Teitelbaum, Stanley H. *Sports Heroes, Fallen Idols*. Lincoln, NE: University of Nebraska Press, 2005.

BIBLIOGRAPHY

Andrews, Luke. "Steroid Prevention the NCAA Way." *Oregon Daily Emerald,* June 9, 2006. Retrieved September 24, 2008 (http://media.www.dailyemerald. com/media/storage/paper859/news/2006/06/09/Sports/Steroid.Prevention. The.Ncaa.Way-2043276.shtml).

Assael, Shaun. "Big Night." ESPN.com, January 21, 2003. Retrieved December 16, 2008 (http://espn.go.com/magazine/vol6no03strongmen.html).

Assael, Shaun. *Steroid Nation: Juiced Home Run Totals, Anti-Aging Miracles, and a Hercules in Every High School: The Secret History of America's True Drug Addiction.* New York, NY: ESPN Publishing, 2007.

Chaikin, Tommy, and Rick Telander. "The Nightmare of Steroids." *Sports Illustrated,* October 24, 1988. Retrieved September 16, 2008 (http://vault. sportsillustrated.cnn.com/vault/article/magazine/MAG1067916/index.htm).

Cheatorbeat.com. "Tony Mandarich." September 30, 2008. Retrieved October 20, 2008 (http://www.cheatorbeat.com/tony-mandarich/football/1117).

DrugStory.org. "Foul Play: Sports, Doping, and Teens: A Roundtable Discussion." Retrieved November 4, 2008 (http://www.drugstory.org/ feature/foul_play.asp).

ESPN.com. "Study Sheds Light on Why Athletes Behave Badly." September 27, 2005. Retrieved September 23, 2008 (http://sports.espn.go.com/espn/ news/story?id=2172121).

Fainaru-Wada, Mark, and T. J. Quinn. "How U.S. Sports Measure up to the 'Gold Standard' of Testing." ESPN.com, May 23, 2008. Retrieved September 28, 2008 (http://sports.espn.go.com/espn/columns/story?id=3408547).

Goldberg, Linn, M.D., et al. "Effects of a Multidimensional Anabolic Steroid Prevention Intervention." *Journal of American Medical Association,* November 20, 1996. Retrieved September 27, 2008 (http://jama.ama-assn. org/cgi/content/abstract/276/19/1555).

Goodwin, Michael. "Drug Use Believed to Extend Beyond Two Schools in South." *New York Times,* January 20, 1985. Retrieved November 4, 2008 (http://

query.nytimes.com/gst/fullpage.html?res=9E0CE6D7143BF933A15752C0A
963948260&sec=health&spon=&pagewanted=all).

Harmon, Dick. "Steroid Scandal Catching Attention of MWC Athletic Trainers."
Deseret Morning News, May 1, 2005. Retrieved December 16, 2008 (http://
findarticles.com/p/articles/mi_qn4188/is_/ai_n14608320).

Hernandez, Monica. "Former Madison Central High Quarterback Pleads Guilty
to Distributing Steroids." WLBT.com, September 17, 2008. Retrieved
September 23, 2008 (http://www.wlbt.com/global/story.asp?s=9028201).

Hinshelwood, Brad. "Track Star Suspended; Refusal to Take Drug Test Leads to
Year-Long Ban for Female Runner." *The Crimson*, November 13, 2007. Retrieved
October 26, 2008 (http://www.thecrimson.com/article.aspx?ref=520699).

Lidz, Franz. "Looking Out for No. 1: Those Frontline Soldiers in the War on
Steroid Abuse—the Pee Collectors—Are Finally Making a Splash." *Sports
Illustrated*, December 22, 2003. Retrieved October 12, 2008 (http://vault.
sportsillustrated.cnn.com/vault/article/magazine/MAG1030900/index.htm).

National Institute on Drug Abuse. "NIDA Announces Multimedia Public
Education Initiative Aimed at Reversing Rise in Use of Anabolic Steroids
by Teens." April 14, 2000. Retrieved September 28, 2008 (http://www.
drugabuse.gov/medadv/00/NR4-14.html).

National Registry of Evidence-Based Programs and Practices. January 2007.
Retrieved October 1, 2008 (http://www.nrepp.samhsa.gov).

NCAA.org. "NCAA Study of Substance Use Habits of College Student-Athletes."
January 2006. Retrieved October 20, 2008. (http://www.ncaa.org).

New York Times. "Sports People: College Football; Steroid Use Reported."
February 20, 1990. Retrieved September 17, 2008 (http://query.nytimes.
com/gst/fullpage.html?sec=health&res=9C0CE0DB123FF933A15751C0
A966958260).

Office of Applied Studies. "Types of Illicit Drug Use in Lifetime, Past Year, and
Past Month Among Persons Aged 12 or Older: Numbers in Thousands,

2006 and 2007." September 4, 2008. Retrieved October 11, 2008 (http://www.oas.samhsa.gov).

Puma, Mike. "Not the Size of the Dog in the Fight." ESPN.com. Retrieved October 16, 2008 (http://espn.go.com/classic/biography/s/Alzado_Lyle.html).

Puma, Mike. "'Roid Rage." ESPN.com, December 23, 2003. Retrieved December 16, 2008 (http://sports.espn.go.com/espn/classic/news/story?page=add_alzado_lyle).

Shelton, Shannon. "Tony Mandarich Comes Clean in Interview, Forthcoming Book." *Detroit Free Press*, October 3, 2008. Retrieved February 2009 (http://www.standard.net/live/144931).

Telander, Rick. "The Big Enchilada." *Sports Illustrated*, April 24, 1989. Retrieved October 3, 2008 (http://vault.sportsillustrated.cnn.com/vault/article/magazine/MAG1068312/index.htm).

USAToday. "Mandarich Admits Steroid Use in Television Interview." September 30, 2008. Retrieved October 21, 2008 (http://www.usatoday.com/sports/football/nfl/2008-09-30-mandarich_N.htm).

WAPT.com. "Former Football Stand-Out Pleads Guilty in Steroid Case." September 18, 2008. Retrieved September 23, 2008 (http://www.wapt.com/news/17475442/detail.html?rss=jac&psp=news).

INDEX

About the Author

Annie Leah Sommers is a writer and editor living in New York. She has a B.A. in English literature from McGill University in Montreal and an M.A. in children's literature from the Center for the Study of Children's Literature at Simmons College in Boston. She is also a certified secondary school English and E.S.L. teacher.

Photo Credits

Cover (bottom left), p. 1 © www.istockphoto.com/Rob Friedman; cover (bottom center), pp. 1, 5 © Donald Miralle/Getty Images; cover, p. 1 (bottom right) © Andy Lyons/Getty Images; cover (background) Shutterstock; pp. 3, 4 © Doug Benc/ Getty Images; p. 6 © www.istockphoto.com/Damir Spanic; p. 7 © Erich Lessing/ Art Resource, NY; p. 8 © Hulton Archives/Getty Images; p. 9 © Bettmann/ Corbis; pp. 10, 15, 23, 34, 35 © www.istockphoto.com; pp. 12, 20 © www. istockphoto.com; pp. 13, 26, 31, 36, 38 © AP Photos; p. 14 © Sergei Supinsky/AFP/ Getty Images; p. 16 © Christian Peterson/Getty Images; p. 18 © Christian Jakubaszek/Getty Images; p. 21 © Bernstein Associates/Getty Images; p. 22 © Neal Preston/Corbis; p. 24 © Mike Powell/Getty Images; p. 28 © www.istockphoto. com/Mitch Aunger; p. 29 © Tasos Katopodis/AFP/Getty Images; p. 32 © Icon Photos; p. 37 © www.istockphoto.com/Christine Richards.

Designer: Nicole Russo; Editor: Christopher Roberts;
Photo Researcher: Marty Levick